Muskrats

Victoria Blakemore

vblakemore.author@gmail.com

Copyright info/picture credits

Cover, Lone Wolf Photography/Shutterstock; Page 3, Seaq68/Pixabay; Page 5, Brian Lasenby/AdobeStock; Page 7, Tom Koerner/USFWS; Page 9, Storyblocks; Pages 10-11, Storyblocks; Page 13, Seaq68/Pixabay; Page 15, kyslynskyy/AdobeStock; Page 17, Christoph/AdobeStock; Page 19, jmrockeman/Pixabay; Page 21, IrynaLinnyk/AdobeStock; Page 23; kees1/Pixabay; Page 25, Sharon Day/AdobeStock; Page 27, Peter Massas/flickr; Page 29, Uryadnikov Sergey/AdobeStock; Page 31, Seaq68/Pixabay; Page 33, Lone Wolf Photography/Shutterstock

Table of Contents

What Are Muskrats?

Muskrats are small mammals. They are members of the **rodent** family. They are related to animals such as voles and lemmings.

Although muskrats are sometimes mistaken for beavers, they are not closely related.

Muskrats get their name from
their musky scent and the fact
that they look like large rats.

Size

Adult muskrats are usually between one and two feet long. Their tail can grow to be another foot long.

Although they are rather long, muskrats do not weigh much. They often weigh between one and four pounds.

Male muskrats and female muskrats are usually about the same size.

Physical Characteristics

Muskrats have two layers of fur. Their outer layer helps to keep them warm. The layer underneath is very thick and waterproof.

They have a long tail that is flattened. It works as a **rudder** which helps them to swim.

Muskrats are usually brown in color. They may have patches of darker fur on their face and feet.

Habitat

Muskrats are found in wetlands such as marshes, rivers, ponds, and swamps.

Places with still or slow-moving water are best for muskrats. They need to be able to move through the water easily. They also prefer areas with lots of plants.

Range

Muskrats are found in most parts of North America.

They are commonly seen in many states, including Washington, Indiana, and Alaska.

Diet

Muskrats are **omnivores**.
They eat both meat and
plants.

Their diet is made up of
plants such as cattails, pond
weeds, and water lilies. They
also eat clams, small fish,
and frogs.

Muskrats use their front paws to hold their food while they eat.

They can **gnaw** at hard plant parts with their front teeth.

13

Muskrats usually bring their food to a special feeding spot they make in the mud and plants.

This is so that they can be safe from predators like otters or bobcats while they are eating.

When muskrats close their mouths, their front teeth are outside. This allows them to **gnaw** on plants underwater.

Communication

Muskrats use mainly scent and sound to communicate with each other.

They are very **territorial**. Muskrats do not like other muskrats getting too close. They mark their area using their special scent gland under their tail.

Muskrats make sounds such as squeaks and squeals. They often use these sounds as warnings if a predator is nearby.

Movement

Muskrats are excellent swimmers. They are able to stay underwater for as long as fifteen minutes. They can swim both forwards and backwards.

Muskrats can swim up to three miles per hour. They may be able to swim faster in short bursts.

Muskrats have back feet that
are **webbed.** Their back feet are
designed to help them swim.

Muskrat Kits

Muskrats usually have between four and eight babies. Their babies may be called kits or pups.

The kits are born blind and hairless. They are able to feed themselves by the time they are about six weeks old.

Muskrat kits grow quickly. They
are fully grown by the time they
are about six months old.

Muskrat Life

Muskrats are social animals that live in family groups. They are not often seen with muskrats that are not in their family.

Most muskrats are **nocturnal**. They are most active at night. In some places, they may also be active during the day.

Muskrats spend a lot of time

eating among the reeds and

grasses.

Muskrat Lodges

Muskrats build large lodges out of stems, leaves, roots, and mud. They have a main nest **chamber**, tunnels, and smaller chambers.

Lodges may also have more than one entrance. This allows muskrats to quickly escape from predators.

Muskrats build their lodges as big as five feet across and four feet tall.

Muskrats are Important

Some people think that muskrats are pests. However, they are actually very important to their environment.

Muskrats eat a lot of plants that grow in the water. They clear a lot of space for other animals that live in and around the water.

Muskrats provide many other animals with a habitat by clearing plants out of the water.

Population

Muskrats are not currently **endangered**. In most places, their populations are **stable**. In some areas, their populations are **declining**.

Disease, habitat loss, pollution, and hunting are the main threats that muskrats are facing.

In the wild, muskrats often live

between three and four years.

Helping Muskrats

Since muskrats eat plants, they can be pests for farmers. They can also cause problems for dams and homes near the water.

People can help keep their property safe from muskrats by keeping water levels steady and high.

Fences and other **barriers** can also be used. This can reduce the chances of **conflict** between people and muskrats.

Pollution can be a problem for muskrats and other animals. By keeping habitats free from **pollutants**, people can make sure that animals have a safe habitat to live in.

Glossary

Barrier: something that blocks the way, a fence or wall

Chamber: a room or compartment

Conflict: fight or strong disagreement

Declining: getting smaller

Endangered: at risk of becoming extinct

Gnaw: to bite or chew on

Nocturnal: animals that are active and night

Omnivore: an animal that eats meat and plants

Pollutant: something that pollutes the air, water, or land

Rodent: small mammals with long front teeth used for gnawing

Rudder: a part used to steer in the water

Stable: steady, unchanging

Territorial: when an animal is protective of its territory

About the Author

Victoria Blakemore is a first grade

teacher in Southwest Florida with a

passion for reading.

You can visit her at

www.elementaryexplorers.com

Also in This Series

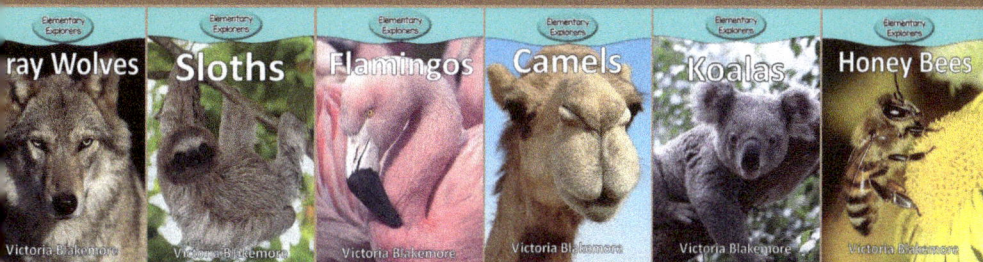

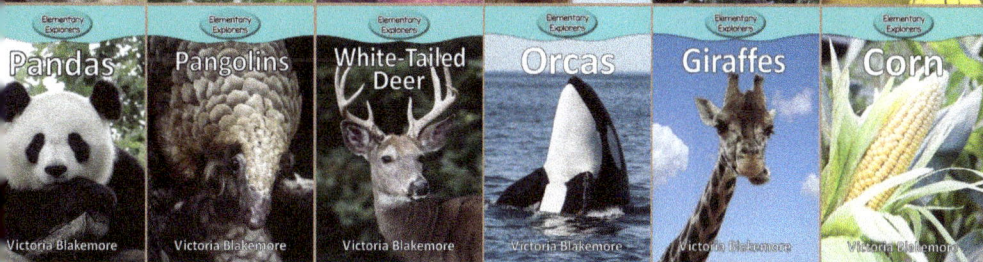

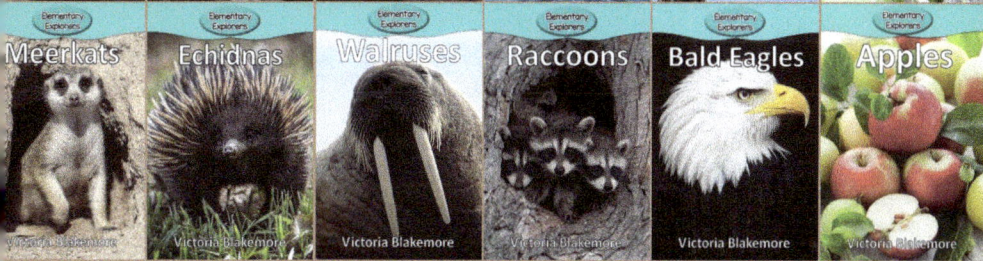

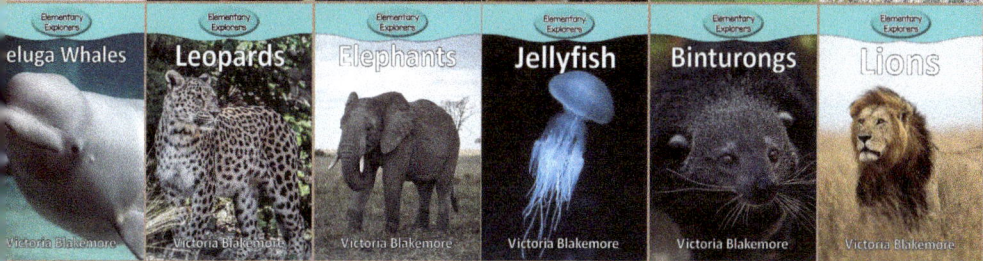

Elementary Explorers

ray Wolves	Sloths	Flamingos	Camels	Koalas	Honey Bees
Victoria Blakemore	Victoria Blakemore	Victoria Blakemore	Victoria Blakemore	Victoria Blakemore	Victoria Blakemore
Pandas	Pangolins	White-Tailed Deer	Orcas	Giraffes	Corn
Victoria Blakemore	Victoria Blakemore	Victoria Blakemore	Victoria Blakemore	Victoria Blakemore	Victoria Blakemore
Meerkats	Echidnas	Walruses	Raccoons	Bald Eagles	Apples
Victoria Blakemore	Victoria Blakemore	Victoria Blakemore	Victoria Blakemore	Victoria Blakemore	Victoria Blakemore
Arctic Foxes	Red Pandas	Cassowaries	Tigers	Ladybugs	Moose
Victoria Blakemore	Victoria Blakemore	Victoria Blakemore	Victoria Blakemore	Victoria Blakemore	Victoria Blakemore
eluga Whales	Leopards	Elephants	Jellyfish	Binturongs	Lions
Victoria Blakemore	Victoria Blakemore	Victoria Blakemore	Victoria Blakemore	Victoria Blakemore	Victoria Blakemore
Dolphins	Reindeer	Hammerhead Sharks	Hippos	Pumpkins	Peafowl
Victoria Blakemore	Victoria Blakemore	Victoria Blakemore	Victoria Blakemore	Victoria Blakemore	Victoria Blakemore

Also in This Series

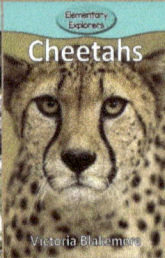

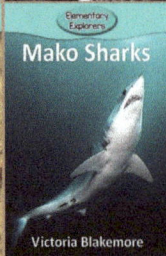

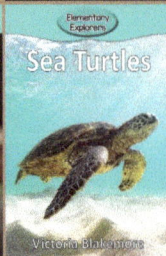

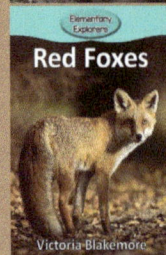

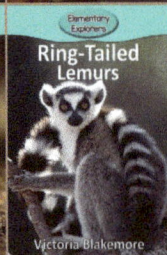

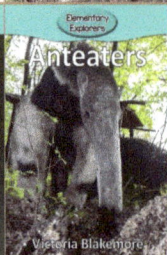

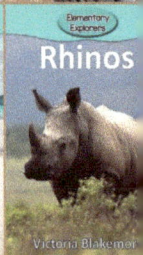

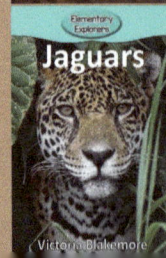

Elementary Explorers — **Chameleons** — Victoria Blakemore

Elementary Explorers — **Florida Panthers** — Victoria Blakemore

Elementary Explorers — **Aye-Ayes** — Victoria Blakemore

Elementary Explorers — **Black Bears** — Victoria Blakemore

Elementary Explorers — **Cheetahs** — Victoria Blakemore

Elementary Explorers — **Manatees** — Victoria Blakemore

Elementary Explorers — **Gingerbread** — Victoria Blakemore

Elementary Explorers — **Polar Bears** — Victoria Blakemore

Elementary Explorers — **Hot Chocolate** — Victoria Blakemore

Elementary Explorers — **Orangutans** — Victoria Blakemore

Elementary Explorers — **Coyotes** — Victoria Blakemore

Elementary Explorers — **Marshmallows** — Victoria Blakemore

Elementary Explorers — **Strawberries** — Victoria Blakemore

Elementary Explorers — **Aardvarks** — Victoria Blakemore

Elementary Explorers — **Mako Sharks** — Victoria Blakemore

Elementary Explorers — **Alligators** — Victoria Blakemore

Elementary Explorers — **Frogs** — Victoria Blakemore

Elementary Explorers — **Hedgehogs** — Victoria Blakemore

Elementary Explorers — **Brown Bears** — Victoria Blakemore

Elementary Explorers — **Bongos** — Victoria Blakemore

Elementary Explorers — **Sea Turtles** — Victoria Blakemore

Elementary Explorers — **Quokkas** — Victoria Blakemore

Elementary Explorers — **Muskrats** — Victoria Blakemore

Elementary Explorers — **Zebras** — Victoria Blakemore

Elementary Explorers — **Red Foxes** — Victoria Blakemore

Elementary Explorers — **Ring-Tailed Lemurs** — Victoria Blakemore

Elementary Explorers — **Platypuses** — Victoria Blakemore

Elementary Explorers — **Anteaters** — Victoria Blakemore

Elementary Explorers — **Kangaroos** — Victoria Blakemore

Elementary Explorers — **Rhinos** — Victoria Blakemore

Elementary Explorers — **Jaguars** — Victoria Blakemore

Elementary Explorers — **Wombats** — Victoria Blakemore

www.ingramcontent.com/pod-product-compliance
Lightning Source LLC
Chambersburg PA
CBHW051252020426

42333CB00025B/3180